AF211375

I would like to thank my mother and friends and others who supported me by listening to my deranged thoughts, deliberately or involuntarily....

Dear reader, don't be afraid to laugh or cry,
I sure have.

I hope my words touch at heart and inspire to creativity.

Late for my coronation

PRINCESSS

Pink princess sheet in the night
making tiny drops on your forehead
Science fiction lives
lies cluttered on top of each other
on the shelf and in your mind

Embraced by a bright red meadow
and a warm orange moon
gently sung to a slumber full of dreams
eager to retell the stories to mom
The last time it happened was this dawn

I see you
but you have not met me yet
unaware, humbled and innocent
someone would go as for to even say pretty
I am someone
I am no one
I was you

Pink princess pressed against your face
suffocated in your golden age
baby of light never has to see the true night
I am protecting you from the lies
be thankful for my gift
it is what saved your life

Magic and spells, all gone
the sacrifices I had to make
for the memory to remain full piece
I had to destroy the princess inside of me

RED

I colored my hair red to match my lips
the fire in me was burning out
I had to spark it to life
rhythmic songs for elves to dance
they strike the drum twice as fast
pumping blood to keep me in trance
flowing of red from toes to head
thick as porridge blocking my veins
no more water in store

I gave it to the peasants to water their fields
I gave it to factories to poison it with chemi-
cals
I gave it to the people to bathe their bodies
but for the most part, it went in tiny boats
drifting typhoons on my cheeks
the salty storm settled by my tongue, once again
thirsty for more

Thirsty for red is the butcher
the vampire
the doctor
my blood is purer than for them to steal
Instead I shall fertilize the soil of the tall
shadows
while looking up to see the crowns they wear so
proudly
embraced by life will be how I end mine

Dearest season
you will jewel my head with amanita and clothe
my body with fallen leaves
when summer comes

the red carpet of my devotees will turn into a
green one
for the guests of your mother garden
however, many seasons will come and go until my
pure white mannequin has endured its last
and a guest I will be no more
but a host fulfilling its quest

MRS. NICE GUY

The red is fading and so am I
the petals are falling of the cherry-tree
as are my eyelashes to repel the beauty queen
inside of me

When summer comes and the leaves turn green and
the children playing by the water stream
when the days are supposed to be light and full
of wonders
no one can notice my thunders
so mrs. Nice guy comes out for everyone's de-
light
for the cash in my wallet
for the trip I will not like
for the future dream
I will never live to see

Glued on smirk and giggle is appreciated by the
men who look down on me
a sheep is what they see
but they can not see the layers of clothing that
hides the mean
only if they knew how easy a prey they are

But I will not reveal their nakedness
because the people do not know yet that my dream
will not come true
so mrs. Nice guy has to stick around for a while

SYMPHONY

Baby trees
growing beside each other
family
connected from roots in symphony
life as long as 203
sweet as a peach
blessed by sunbeams
dressed in green with melody of gymnopedié no. 1

Soothing cradle back and forth
wind humming the lullaby of the old north
not even half grown yet
just learned to take its first steps
yet more alive and blossomed than I will ever
become
in scornful pleasure they look at me and laugh
humbled I keep walking as the dreadful human I
have been cast as

Suddenly one sluggish tree takes me by surprise
he looks different from the others
brown and downcast
he whispers in my ear
"don't worry my dear,
they are just happy to be here,
my time has come even in this life,
may I pray for you to take my place when the mo-
ment is near"

203, and each one of the trees are being shopped
down in their prime
the song of the trees is overused and old cra-

203, and each one of the trees are being chopped
down in their prime
the song of the trees is overused and old cra-
ving new hits that would last in centuries to
come
a blank notepaper with ink that has not yet
dried will fill its surface with a song of a new
world waiting to come undone

Fresh meat is planted on their graves
it is I who lead the funeral choir
for I waited my whole life never again to look
down at the ground
my fetus will seed amongst others waiting to be
freed
high in the clouds singing together
symphony after symphony

SILENCE

Every digging hole of problem filled with cement
rhymes crash into shred
leave me alone mister theft!
stealing my thoughts and my last breath
I am supposed to be the raging storm of the west

So why am I the lake where swans nest?
where the pure reflections of the sky in the wa-
ter will make any man go insane
where the sounds of the soft breeze will make
any rockers' ears bleed

White noise is no longer soothing
only deceiving my senses
I wonder where I left them
back in the eight-year-old memory of a girl that
is fading
or hidden deep inside of me waiting to be freed
nightmare would be if they have left
eternally

Anyway, pondering though the night will not make
everything alright
the birds have started singing outside
how long has it been for this to coincide?

Silence makes music in the night
but people get tired of music after awhile

A QUEEN'S BIRTHRIGHT

Being a queen is hard
    since twenty-three hours a day
            you are not

you cannot sleep in a qeen size bed
         join the homeless on the street!

you cannot have a tiara
        throw a paperbag over your head!

ou cannot be served a royal diner
            eat your neighbor's garbage!

MOTHER

I wish my mother was dead
so that I could love her
so that I could see her beautiful big smile on
that face that even in her older days always had
a child's gaze

So that I could appreciate all the things she
has done for me
and remember how her hair looked like golden th-
reads in the sun and like big waves when in the
wind
so that I could remember her with her friends,
laughing and chatting and being an actual human
being, instead of my mother

I want to remember the person she is when I am
not there to pick at her flaws or draw out the
monster inside her with my own monster claws
I wish I was not born so that she could have a
life without my misery, without my hands pushing
her down into the water as she drowns

This is my first time experiencing life and I am
sorry the simple existence is too much for me
and that I would rather die
I am sorry that the matches she gives will not
light up the night
my fire is already out and no kindling in the
world could make a sparkle strike

But who will light her fire when her matches are
out?
when she has given all to mine
but my wood is soaked in self pity
too damp to light
so it was all in vain I am afraid

I am afraid sometimes that she does know who I
am
that the mysterious facade is transparent
what if I am a book hidden in plain sight
and she is the only one who could read its insi-
de?
What if we are so alike but choose to disguise
it due to fright?

I see my own mortality in the wrinkles on her
cheeks
my humanity that unveils in her caving physique
and it scares the shit out of me
her vulnerability is what I hate
but in the dungeons of my heart valves
crave

hers is wide open
naked and ready to be touched
while mine only comes out as a blue shade strok-
ing my face gently
then pushed away

Maybe that is why I wish my mother dies
because I want the same for me in the end
to be remembered for my smile and glowing hair
in the sun

to be an icon of tragical daughters
and a haunting thought for mourning mothers and
fathers
to never grow up suffering the same existence of
my mom
that of having a daughter
who is a time bomb

The mere idea of her
makes me love with such an ache
it is painful
she is spring in my winter bear pit
green leaves and blossoming flowers
teeth bright that burn the retina
dimples that politely grope her skin
like the crisp breeze kissing your neck
making shivers down your spine

Bright salmon aura infecting everyone and eve-
rything she touches like a virus
my useless antidote does not work
it being fabricated by guilt
guilt of my true heart wanting her touch
the natural itch longing for beauty
sure, does true beauty hurt
sometimes, the eyes you'll have to avert

BLUE HYDRANGEAS

I own a tiny garden
outside my tiny house
in my tiny garden I grow fake flowers
except my blue hydrangeas
that I water with Ultraviolence

The fake flowers invade my life
plastic covered lies everywhere I see
at least the hydrangeas glow blue in the night
aqua blue shadowed truth
shades of cool
serum of youth

My garden is a sacred place
my very own child
one day of water in the vase
means another day the plants grow wild

The flowers rot
so will I
them confident in tomorrow
so am I

CAMOUFLAGE

Clothes piling up
like a mountain of garbage
I am a snail with new shells everyday
abundance of responsibilities
underneath the dump
dirty clothes camouflage my decay

Conceal the worries in a box
in my drawer of socks
each sunrise I look at my faults
close it for a day of synthetic orthodox

Do me one favor
never to open the bell jar
once my outfits have ended
my self-disarming trailer
needs to survive in tales
once I have descended

AFFECTION

At the dance floor, in my splendor, purple
lights flashing my face while
I'm flashing them with my beauty
I notice them noticing me
my flesh
cream porcelain innocence
pulsating veins and broken spine
do they notice my desperation?
because I have started to notice it too

Who said that loneliness was a bad thing?
yeah, that's right, my mind
so I clutch on to every find
store them in my dresser beside robes and night-
gowns
certain nights the treasures I put on
and recollect the feeling of being their consi-
deration
just for a minute of affection

Faceless hunters looking for prey
reindeer in the open bush sensing a fall out of
nowhere
let me make it easy and hunt me when the moon is
out
on a clear night my visions blur
once the dawn comes
my sights once again occur
and I'm no longer blind

That is when the real nightmares haunt my mind
they depict a movie about womenkind
refined by its anthem

the walk of shame
carrying such heavy weight of guilt in my arms
it brakes my bones and I fall into the abyss
the stages of insanity has cracked my remiss

They will glue my bones together but it will
always end in a crack
cracking bones squeaking on the dance floor
a birdsong for those who will do me wrong
infinite loop on and on and on

THE ROOM

Amongst empty wine glasses
there it is, the last drop of the day
miserably it waits to be emptied and join the
hollow parade
don't mind me sitting here in frustration
I suckle on midnight evaluation
the room screams of family gatherings, reunions,
parties, overall cognation
I hate it with all my body

My halo above is nothing but a lamp
shade of yarn crafted by a knitter
I envision the wine turns to liquor
I poor it over the lamp and watch memories turn
bitter
as the flames flicker

the lamp would be cherished on walls for decades
If I was a painter
but I do not trust other peoples' lies
so, I cannot paint
instead, I write
preferably the withering of everyday life
today a room
tomorrow eternity's doom
no judgement in a diary
I presume

Little angels fly out with every cough
little devils suck on to my throat
they lay eggs and infect my brain
hatred spreads fast in this hell hospitable en-
vironment
I am like a welcoming reception for demon resi-
dents

Tired, sick, and dehydrated
my symptoms could start a band
their background dancers,
self-pity and gloom
their first show would be in this dim room
their name would be Radiohead

Five meters outside and this would be a happy
poem
about the singing of the waves hitting the
cliffs
about the full moon, painting bright spots on
the black canvas
about the beautiful breeze in the night
but I refuse to breath fresh air

Therefore, I sniff in my thoughts as oxygen or
cocaine
what is even the difference?
a room stuffed with question marks layered like
lasagna in the process of my thoughts
is the lasagna vegetarian?
all I do is gorge in overthinking
can you get suffocated from words?
If so, I am as ripe as a blueberry in June

Even the silence of these walls can not mute the
echoes of my original tune
everywhere I go
I sit in this room

To you I talked more
that late night my throat was sore
but tall tales I swore

Pine needles of hair
attempt to touch me and die
hedgehog quills of spine

SEASON OF THE WITCH

Ocean season is over
no more seashells washing ashore
being dragged with the waves
choking on foam like a whore

except I was not a whore
I was the little mermaid walking on broken
glass, who didn't stop once my feet were sore
for no more than a man
a man I will feel sympathy for no more
no more

I am tired of the red curls getting in my face
of the saltwater making my eyes red and swell
I will dye my hair black velvet
and gather all my friends
to a brunch on my burial
the old me is dead
I have got to pick up every stitch
cause it is the season of the witch

I am tired of living in stress
a timid girl gets nothing she earns for
a seductress lives to cause distress
it liberates her sole core
life is a war and testosterone is the nemesis
so, it is written in the sorceress genesis

I have my own musketeer
my cat who is called Aramis
the only man who maintains gentility
although, his lack of balls is a lack of virili-
ty
possibly the reason for his nobility

Me and my girls playing hand in glove with the
rival
it is a game for sure
eating men on a stick is our new gamble

As we devour their intestines and gurgle on
their blood as a bottle of merlot
in moonlight we radiantly glow
dancing with the shadows on tiptoe
casting spells everywhere we go

BUSHES

Walking alongside the rusty fence
built the same time as the decaying houses
the brick walls were unfortunately immense
in the days of political mice

Do step in
into winter's cold furiture
here is your queue
wait in line for your problems to vanish
the magical words - merci beaucoup

Stumble on icy varnished floors
match these hands that trace snowflakes
back to the bricks imprisoning inmates
keep out whatever filth you can carry

Lines and colors to confuse the blind
corridors never reaching the horizon
a place beyond time
sinking over humankind
them flow over the floors of amazon
an instinctive, determined goal
them swimming fishes in a shoal

On my way from the den
feeling as empty as ever
greetings with the fence once again
where my feet stand there are bushes in the sand
capitated limbs try to reach for the sky without
luck
On the other side of the fence
their siblings strive
for on doctors' praise they suck

Is that what hospitals are all about?
watering
filling soil
nurturing the field
so once your healed
they will cut you down
just to be mean

The bricks call on me
I want to go back inside
where silence completes
nothingness meats
I can crawl up in a corner
watch the tide cease

I AM NOT A POET

Marshmallow dipped forest
blue ufo flashes the film screen
Scully and Mulder are nowhere to be seen

It may be Rudolph's glowing nose
that arrived early this year
disoriented by unseasonable snow
he thought Christmas might be near

The car passes by quickly and disappears into
the night
and I, a reindeer turn my head and stare at the
magical sight
trying to capture every drop of momentary light

To get the best vision of all
I squint my eyes and keep the pupils at stands-
till
spruces blurre into a smudgy wall
I picture this my final glimpse in this world

A picture will not capture its essence
even if you would stand right beside me and see
it with your very own eyes
you would not see it through mine

The notable artist has always been narcissistic
in their ways
but my writing is not even okay
Am I worthy of these eyes
that trail the beautiful maze?

Stepping in the deep snow feels like the great
jump I've never dared
it is not enough
so, I lay myself totally bared
with a thud, the falling stops

Finally, a quiet tomb
in this position I do my squinting trick and the
freezing cold warms my heart
wishing this my final bedroom

I am not a photographer
I am not a poet
I am an artist

I see the eloquent details that hide between the
lines of marshmallow dipping
words are cheap with their tipping
nonetheless, the closest to
emotional stripping

SYLVIA PLATH

I will follow your path
Sylvia Plath
not tomorrow, not yet
but as soon as I forget
that is what I was thinking this eve
when I had struggled to leave my worries behind
me
like a man with a rope around his neck strugg-
ling in the air
still exhaling nonetheless
with a disappointment in every breath

I had planned everything, but it didn't go as I
planned
steaming water
candles
the "easy classical piano" playlist
everything on the damn list
the mission was to make it dissolve like Doreen
my angst slipping through my fingers like mer-
cury
alternate psychology for someone sedentary

Problem was
the time it took to set everything perfect the
roller coaster had already reached its high
my mediative mind said goodbye
I felt as crucified

Regardless of the wind that swept me off my feet
I dipped my crown in the tub and began to rub
but I came to the realization that to remove my
sins
is to rub away my skin and to skim off my blood

my impurity resists deep in the mud

Therefore, I stopped the carving and instead
slowly sank into the mud
an unnerving feeling poked at my nerves
a forged memory of before I was even birthed
stuck in fetal position
in juice I felt like preserves

Dictionary's birth grabbed me in by a chain
the key for the birth I craved
had slipped down the drain
I drowned while reaching for the keyhole
letting the sins mercifully poison my soul

Perhaps I am not Esther nor will I ever be
perhaps my teenage angst needs the reaction
with banking against the walls
fleeing with the stars
music in my eardrums' brawls
humiliate every part with my fresh scars

SO LONG

Did your mind crack as Lisa's from psych?
or as the heavy feet on uncertain ice
when I walked right over you
I blame the moon
leo sun Leo moon
how could you let me be this blue

Starlight gaze in your eye
but I looked at the stars in the night sky
my shallow heart cannot take your love to the
grave
For I would have been trapped in a cave
digged by my own hands
drugged by your fairy lands
captivated in trance

Walking barefoot on searing sand
on the beaches of Tuscany
with a drink in my hand
I found I was still as hollow as a bone
and my tear duct being stripped from clothes

You should know
melancholy is my second home
she is the only one to fill my dome
I used to see you as my brother from another
mother
now you are someone other
with reason
So long, lover

FOR YOU

Fuck you and your soft touch
for you I starve
for you to feel my bones and knuckles

For you I bend and pull
twist and rearrange
making knots with my limbs
for you to play your little game
unravel them

For you I slow down my heartbeat
rhythmically march on the edge
never scared of the height
existing solely on breathing the same oxygen as
the clouds

For you I pretend my locks curl in pretzels
for you to brush them out flat and dull
while I lay on your chest paralyzed like a door
mat

For you I spiritless sway in circles
a broken record stuck on loop
vibrations pass on to you

The reason
for strolling on the verge
is not for you to catch me when I fall
it is so I can crack my skull open

The reason
I do not eat is not because you can weightlessly
carry me to the moon

it is so I can slowly evaporate into thin air

The reason I cyclically spin
hips movingly in directions you are in
is not for you to pair up in a pirouette
it is so my loins can burn up as fast as a ciga-
rette
in swirl my toes leave the earth
and every cell rebirth

Fuck you
for making me pretend to care
and for imagining myself I do not

APPLE

Sitting outside with an emptiness inside
my hunger can never be satisfied

I pick up
I drink up
I lick up the last on my plate

I pity
I dread
I loathe in self hate

In the garden of Eden which I call home
something ungodly revokes
yet kin to the Eve we know

Do I have her to blame for my impulsive habits?
is it our womanly nature to gulp while ashamed?

gulp in jewelry
in dress
in men
and in bread
oh, I have hit bottom
now conservative pondering has me embedded

The serpent tempts and I do not prevent
for I have no license of my own will
but in bed I wept as I could feel my mouth rot-
tening and I chewed on my teeth like bubblegum
the forbidden fruit has my obedience for I suc-

cumb

In the evening newscast they claim
war is over
but the morning news tells a different story
about how troops round up
because war is over if you want it
And I am too hungry to decide for myself

In the morning it shows again
the hole
empty as before
all attempts worthless
put me on a trial for betrayal
in prison hopefully I can rot in a cell
prison food would do the trick, I tell

Anyhow, not to be boringly sane or anything
but maybe I should go and take a cold shower
rinse the thoughts down my back and down the
drain they go
look at the unnervingly dull bathroom tiles some
kind of grey shade that whisper calm words
hugged for a bedtime story in a land where bodi-
es are
anatomy
biology
mythology

CHRISTMAS

Merry joyful forthcoming
Mary of Nazareth brings celibacy cunning
marry me to a torso of dirt
Marie Antoinette chugs on desert

Bring light into dark alleys
poke with a stick on bruises she carries
stuff bloated bellies with homemade goodies
feel the potatoes squirm pass the entrance
taste the sour aroma of Christmas meals

Chant the cheerful hymn in solitude
wish upon a star your eardrums bust
thickness of red produce bloody lewd

I care little to none about gifts this year
no materialistic junk will give clarity
neither will it transport me up or down I fear
yet nothing will stop me
from licking Christianity's balls in
insanity

GHOST

My ghost is not like yours
it is not scary or haunted
it does not stand in a dark corner
for it to be admired from afar

My ghost is kind and familiar
my ghost is present in the open
even though the sun rays hurt its frail white
cloak, it does as it's told
and follows me everywhere
both day and nighttime

When I surprise it
 my ghost jumps up and down
and then whimpers as a small child
my ghost is scared

That is why I will take it bowling next week
and the week after that, we will be camping near
the ocean
I will look after it
my ghost is not like yours

WISHES ON EYELASHES

A perfectly fallen eyelash
on a pitiful index
a hurricane producing a crash
without any effects

A wish to disappear into the night
considering this slice of a moon shrunken to a
dried prune
can be the loophole out of this endless fight

the tiny moon does not want to leave its suite
balancing its light form on a pointy seat
drowned in a salt wave from a thundering rave
blue clouds in the heavens above
produces what may be known as a drug

dried off on soft fabric then thrown in a pile
on the floor
only seconds that lasts and it is ignored
wishes rewrite
an eyelash' broken destiny
string of light
it disappears into the night

Dissect me please
pick me   apart
   piece by piece
study my disease

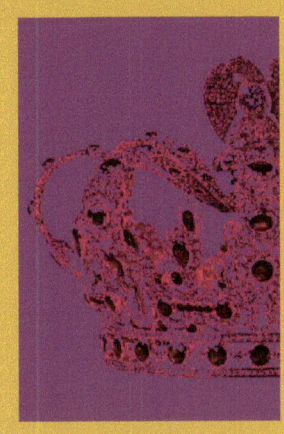

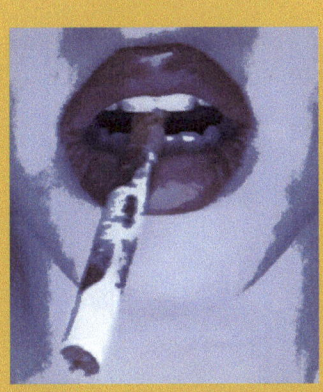

REGLA

I am condemned by the gods to love you
before our screaming souls opened their eyes to
this world
I prepared the journey of loving you eternally
I breath so I can digest the same air as you
knowing our connected souls will never reach
mortality
my heart swallowed by the waves of Poseidon
amongst fens and pearls I glance up at the hori-
zon
in the sun your true life form lies
from hibernation I rise
sunstrokes passing warmth
flying to your light like a moth

Oh, great misery
I should be held accountable for grieving your
evanescense
when all I need to survive is appreciate your
presence
I will soul cycle our bond beyond the grave
so that I will never have to walk torments pave
never miss your soft voice
never have to feel enslaved by my own solitude
even as a corpse I will not notice my hollow bo-
nes
because inside of me a clone of venus roams
your dark locks that embody a familiar warmth

PRETTY

I am no longer pretty when I cry
at least my hair stays up
a lion mane of gold needles
careful not to poke at my skin

From distance I glow with plump cheeks
nevertheless, with the tip of my nose against
the cool surface of the mirror
I can see through my pores into my skull where a
white ghost appears
luminous behind the pink brick wall of face

All that is left is a numb vibrating energy that
I cannot find the source of
it is everywhere and nowhere
in a pocket of my heart
in a pulsating aura
in every cell

I bask in the passion of it
my first love
gently it seduces
on the bruises it causes it kisses
as my dear friend describes
there is no devotion without abuses

I bask in the tension of it
like an astronaut floating lightly in the press-
ured vacuum of space
letting the black hole swallow me whole, stretch
me out like jam on a piece of bread
hugs so tight they strangle the soul
while my face turns blue, and my visions enfold
I uphold a grin

laughing with chagrin
for the pressure is a comforting sin

I bask in the force of it
powerfully domineeringly it takes over my will
I gladly allow it
a slow yet precise kill

The it, is neither questioned nor analyzed
for outside my door is a welcome rug for it to
step inside
invited for a cup of tea and destruction of my
furniture
without my invited vandal who am I to be?
when the cup is empty who am I to drown in the
sea?
as the years pass by who am I to believe
in the sole aim of existing in piece?

WOMEN

His shoulders rose high
a mountain of bullshit
light smirk on his lips
the young boys must think he has wit

Frightening man
ignorant man
successful man
ape-man

His thesis
that men succeeded more often to unalive them-
selves
as an argument they are the better species
then the weak women failing
since they have hope to see land
in the storm they are sailing

Women are born with suffering
the onset from our birth when we hear our mother
cry
the first dart hitting the bullseye
we're reminded of our future pain
one we must get by

The second dart hits right at heart
pigtails and innocence blend with adult villai-
ness
horrifying scenes with blood between the knees
a new journey joining the women army
every month a new casualty
The third dart comes in shadow as heaven
but it turns out it is just another lesson
a boy admiring one's womanly features
that is what love is about, yells the preachers

our own voice is already burnt-out
we have no choice
but to fake thy rejoice

The dart that gives the longest applaud
is the beautiful fraud
tearing every woman apart
created by an act of God
he had an ace up his sleeve
the only people he had to conceive
was Adam and Eve
and even in that state, he did not have a due
date

All the rapid darts make it impossible to duck
we stand wounded in crossfire
ready for the next stike
carrying the total remains of history's gunfire
our strength comes from seeing the holes on the
punctured bodies
their fight even worse than ours
to surrender is to burn their memoirs

Women feel death everyday
As we bleed from our bodies
Give birth in pain

We feel it within in a different way

We feel it so it hurts
we feel it as mundane
we feel it in love
constant chest pains

A wife

a mother
the magic two I will never cover
still deep inside I wonder
if those really are the stakes of womanhood
a developed society with a medieval livelihood
that is the definition of irony

LUCKY

Lucky is the right word I guess
I should be lucky to have a mind as beautiful as
mine
mesmerising melodies
pictures of my own design
being able to fantazise whatever
create forever
unlimited aestethics for individual pleasure
it makes no difference whatsoever

If not in use for fear of letting loose
I deserve nothing but abuse
too much in that walnut organ
expectations of creativity does not fit reality
my brain is smudged from shooting myself with a
gun

Therefore I use my escape route with blue lights
sirens streak my face as if I have been found
out
but I am still in hiding, under the sheets, in a
shell of dunes
my existence echoes of clues

Time goes by and seconds become hours when you
loose track of time
my limbs dissolve into the cushions
the camouflage I wanted so
turns out to be the end of my soul
an eclipse from myself

what I thought was instictive running from pro-
blems towards solitude
was instead running away from the only love that
was left
my brain still stewed

Who am I to be judged?
People of all centuries have been avoiding
troubles through easy getaway's
foundation of the human hays
will I ever have a relaxation that does not make
me more exhausted?
will I ever overcome the obstacles of creation?

I WANT

I do not want to exist in this body
in this mind
oh, if I only disembody
only then can I conquer the spellbind

My branches desire to grab stars in their palms
but I am stuck with these arms
that cannot even take me to mars
even if it was possible with flying cars

My roots crave the inedible
the sweet tooth of a five-year-old
Adult life tastes chemical
decomposed garbage wrapped in gold

Take me back to when concepts of existence did
not rule my entire existence
to when the sun crested in the east and settled
in the west
to when the sun setting in the west was not a
reminder of this immortal test
to when time was a measure of playtime
ticking down for a nurturing rest
now I am riding horses with my hands tied
so fast, my future is already behind

To when senses presented themselves naturally
in the innocent biological vitality
the morning smell of coffee and sounds ratt

ling from the kitchen downstairs
white foam swallowing tangled hair on the beach
sand between toes
following a goose in the blank sky wherever it
goes

Memories memories let me sink into you
exist there in a tiny vacuum where I can remem-
ber
notes from the past breath me
melancholy drives the hearts center

When you die you cannot see sunsets
although the sunsets do not taste the same as
before
when you die you forget
I want to remember the sunsets evermore

I want to live again and again and again
from the beginning
not to the end

PEACE

With my clickity-clack I roam the halls of the
open road
Asphalt bends before me as I step on its grave
Everywhere is my kingdom
I am the pioneer
the navigator
the explorer
The eyeball surrounded by shiny sweat drops in
the sky
hums along to my tune and follow me wherever
Deep in the forest under pines and snarling bus-
hes
Wide eyed on yellow meadows crooked from earths'
orb
Here, knowledge becomes bliss
Inhaling steaming fresh air makes my true life
form appear
An anthropoid creature vigorously sprinting
Swaying in the wind
Transforming to the texture of natures creations
The landscape gracefully caress my soul
And I am the landscape
I grew up on these hills
I know their vast courtesy
This is where I belong

© Nora Svensson 2023
Förlag: BoD – Books on Demand, Stockholm,
Sverige
Tryck: BoD – Books on Demand, Norderstedt,
Tyskland
ISBN: 978-91-7969-666-5